PAROS
ANTIPAROS

EDITIONS
TOUBI'S ®
ΕΚΔΟΣΕΙΣ

ATHENS 1998

Text: GEORGE KOUKAS
Photo: G. VOGIATZIS, G. YIANNELOS, G. KOUMOUROS
Editing: G. VOGIATZIS

Photosetting, colour separations, montage, publishing:
M. TOUBIS GRAPHIC ARTS S.A., Athens -Tel. no. 9923874, TELEX: 224660

Contents

Paros, in the Cyclades is the island of light:
white, blinding light which stamps on the mind of the visitor the impression
of this brushstroke of nature.
   This island, full of history, lives today with the memory of its brilliant civilisation,
with the nobility of its inhabitants, with the dazzling light which floods it,
and with the intricate lace-work of beaches which surround it.

Entrance to the cave of Antiparos. Lithography done around the end to th

18th Century. (Choiseul - Gouffier, Voyage Pittoresque de la Grèce, 1782-1822).

Aghia Kali - Naoussa

Geographical Position

The island group of Paros-Antiparos lies roughly at the centre of the Cyclades, between Naxos and Sifnos, and 90 nautical miles from Piraeus.

Paros has a surface area of 1,865 square kilometers, with 120 kilometrs of coastline. In the middle of the island is the highest point —the peak of the mountain Aghios Ilias or Aghii Pantes— reaching 771 metres.

The greater part of the coastline is steep and rocky, broken by small, sandy beaches. Only on the eastern side of the island does one find really long, golden beaches. The two large natural bays of the island —of Paroikia and Naoussa— have, however, beautiful, protected sandy beaches.

The ground of the island is rocky, consisting mainly of granite with limestone pockets containing marble. Natural vegetation is rather sparse, with most of the island's flora concentrated inland in the mountainous region where there is water. In the southeast, where the land is flat, one finds large fertile plains under cultivation.

The climate of Paros is temperate, influenced by the annual winds (the 'meltemia') typical of the Central Aegean. The winters are mild, with temperatures rarely below freezing. The summers are cool, with strong winds and long, dry periods. These annual northerly and northeasterly winds, can be very strong, reaching 7 Beaufort, and with a frequancy of 55 percent. They blow predominantly throughout August. In the Spring (May), south easterly winds prevail. The average temperature for the year is 18.5 degrees centigrade (winter, 12 C summer, 25 C). The average sea temperatures are: February, 15.1; May, 18.3 C; August, 24.4 C; November, 19.4 C.

Paros is one of the most fertile islands in the cyclades. It's products are: Wine —arlready known in historic times— oliveoil, potatoes and cereals. The quarries, producing the white parian marmor, are also known since old historic ages. The island plains, which are Naoussa, Marmara, Drouos and Pounta are located in the coastal areas.

Antiparos has a surface area of 38 square kilometres (lenghth, 125 kilometres; width, 5.5 kilometres). The highest point on the island is 300 metres, on the mountain Prophet Ilias. The island has deposits of iron ore, lead and zinc, the mining of which ceased long ago.

The cave of Antiparos

Kolimbithres

PAROS - ANTIPAROS

ΥΠΟΜΝΗΜΑ – LEGEND – MEMORANDUM – LÉGENDE

Οδός Ασφαλτοστρωμένη Asphalt road Asphaltierte Straße Route Asphaltée Strada asfaltata	Οδός σε κακή κατάσταση Road in poor condition Straße in schlechtem Zustand Route en mauvais état Strada in cattivo stato	Αεροδρόμιο Airport Flughafen Aéroport Aeroporto	Κάστρο Castle Schloss Château Castello
Οδός μη Ασφαλτοστρωμένη Non - Asphalt road Nicht - asphaltierte Straße Route non - asphaltée Strada non asfalata	Αρχαιολογικός χώρος Archaeological site Archaeologische Stötte Site archeologique Luogo archeologico	Σπήλαιο Gave Grotte Grotte Grotta	Μοναστήρι Monastery Kloster Monastére Monastero

Spile
Archilo

Akr. Agios Fokas

PAROS
(PAROIKIA)

N. DIPLA   N. KAVOURAS

Askimpelon
Peponas
Agia Eirini   Pithion   Kaloge
N
Akr. Vorino

Keraki

ANTIPAROS   210
Sotires   Monastiri Christou Dasous
STROGYLONISI   Psychopiana
136

Pounta
Glysidia
Petaloudes
335

O r m o s   L i v a d
Kanalia
K A M P R O S
133
Panagia   Agios Nikolaos   Kamboi
Akr. Kalogeros
Venetia
M
A
Akr. Trachilos   Agios Antonios   Voutakos   Kamari
A
G   Karavi
I
300   O
S   Spileo
Stalaktiton
Moni
Ormos Despolikou   I
L   Akr. Akakos
I   TOURNA
A
Akr. Koutsouras   S   PREZA
208   Akr. Makrya Myti   Angairia
305
Ormos Peramataki
GLAROPODA
Akr. Mastichi   TIGANA   O r m o s   A l y k i s
Alyki
Ormos Sostis   Akr. Mirona   Akrotiri
Moni Phaneromeni
N. PANDROS
Trypiti
Kavos Skylos   Akr. Mavros

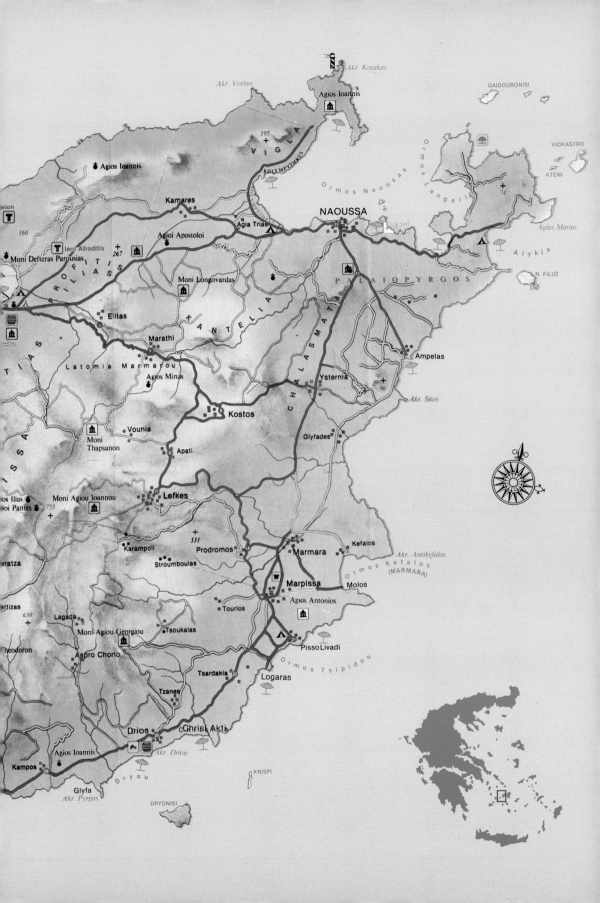

Like all the other Cyclades, Paros began to play its part in the history of the area with the rise of the great naval powers of the eastern Mediterranean. When the great naval state based in Crete came to dominate the area, Paros was important as one of the empire's outposts. At that time, Crete ensured safe communication and transport of minerals between the kindgdoms of Egypt, Babylon, Assyria and the Balkan states. The Minoans found that Paros had safe harbours to offer them, and its central position in the Cyclades made it of strategic importance. This blend of safe harbours and fertile plains round them made the island into a major naval station.

Of these harbours, Paroikia faces the Peloponnese and Naousa faces north, while Drios is opposite Naxos, and the island as a whole lies on the route to Rhodes and Asia Minor. The importance of the military and communications role played by Paros in the Minoian empire is shown by the name the Cretans gave it: Minoa, which was a title of honour given only to royal cities.

According to mythology, the island's first colonist was the Minoan Alcaios, who built the first city on the site on which Paroikia stands today. After the departure of the Minoans, the island was settled by Ionians who had left mainland Greece when the Dorians descended from the North in about 1100 B.C.

The island was still in the hands of the sons of Minoa when the Ionians arrived (the sons' names are recorded as being Eurymedon, Chrysos, Niphalion and Philolaos). After initial defeats, the Ionians subjugated the island, and then proceeded to sack it, destroying the Cretan civilisation and murdering the Cretans themselves. However, archaeological discoveries have shown the extent to which Paros had developed during the Minoan period.

Archaic period

A little later, about a thousand years before the birth of Christ, a band of Arcadians under a leader known as Paros arrived on the island. They were fleeing from the depredations of the same Dorians who had forced the Ionians to seek refuge on Minoa some hundred years before, as the Dorians had by this time extended their way down into the Peloponnese. There were only a few of these Arcadians, but their influence seems to have been strong enough for the former Cretan colony to change its name to Paros, the name of the Arcadian leader. Thus the great maritime, military and commercial base lost its last connection with the Minoans - its name.

As time passed, the inter-marriage of Arcadians and Ionians produced a race which was both clever and active. They developed the island's agriculture, and expanded on to the

Prehistoric finds from Paros and the island Despotico. (First Cycladic Period; middle of the 3rd m. B.C.).

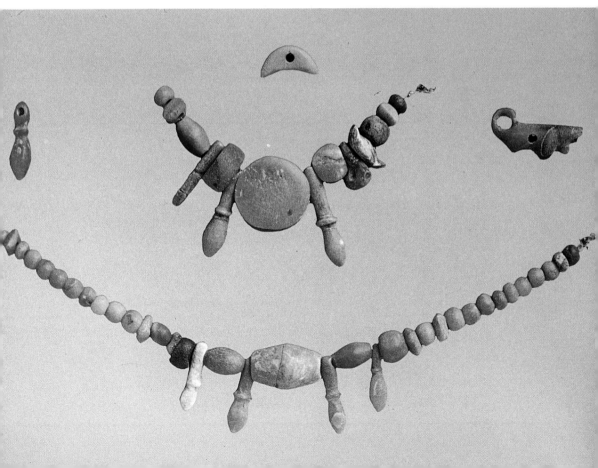

neighbouring island of Antiparos, which was then called Oliaros. During this period, the Parians were worshippers of the goddess Demeter, to whom they dedicated a large temple built on the highest point of the Acropolis of Paroikia, where the church of St. Constantine stands today. Trade began to develop between the Parians and the Phoenicians. The Parians had to offer their famous marble, which was known for its brilliance and its colour. The wealth the island gained from this trade gradually allowed it to develop into a major maritime power. By the 8th century B.C., the Parians controlled sea communications in the Aegean, in the North and along the coast of Thrace. The island's population grew, social classed were created, and the Parians extended their activities into illegal commerce -piracy. Their raids and the slave trade that resulted from them made Paros into a well-known centre for the buying and selling of human life.

Classical, Hellenistic and Roman periods

In their advance towards the rich mineral deposits of the Balkan peninsula, the Parians set up their first colony off the coast of Thrace. In 708 B.C., a group of Parians colonised the island of Thasos, which was rich in deposits of various metals, and excavations in Thasos have brought to light an altar dedicated to Telesicles, leader of the Parian colonsits. He was the father of Archilochus, who after a youth spent as a pirate and mercenary, turned to poetry, where his work won him more admiration from his contemporaries than had his previous activities. The Parians also set up other colonies, such as Galipsos, near Pangaio, Aisymi, Daton, Strymi near Maroneia and Parion in the Hellespont, where the Turkish city of Kemer stands today. They also founded a colony at Paros, on the Dalmatian coast of the Adriatic, on what is today the Yugoslavian island of Hvar.

During this period, the Parians became involved in wars with Naxos (7th century B.C.) and Athens (5th century B.C.). At the same time, strong Ionian and Aeolean communities were set up in the area, and this severely limited the influence of Paros.

In the 6th century, Naxos replaced Paros as the centre of power in the Cyclades, and the aristocratic regime of Naxos was instrumental in the overthrow of democratic government on the rival island. During a period which is notable for conflict between the democratic and oligarchic forms of government, it was only natural that war should break out between the two islands and continue for many years.

This was the point at which a new force entered the scene in the Eastern Mediterranean - the Persians, who, under Cyrus, had conquered all their neighbouring countries and reached the shores of Aegean in Asia Minor. The Naxiot aristocrats,

who had recently been defeated by the democrats, turned to the Persians for help, and this was soon forthcoming. It took the form of a fleet and army under the command of the general Megabates, who arrived off the islands with the intention of restoring the aristocrats to power. The authorities of Paros -aristocratic, as it happened- welcomed the Persians with open arms, and the island became their base in the Aegean. During the Persians' first campaign against mainland Greece, in 490, under Dates, part of the Parian army took ship with the would-be invaders. They aided the Persians in the destruction of Eretria and then took part in the landing at Marathon, where they fought beside the Persians and were defeatd with them. The Athenians never forgave the Parians for this, and soon after Marathon an Athenian army under Miltiades launched an attack on Paros. The attack would have been successful if it had not been for the fact that Miltiades hesitated to launch the final assualt - even though he was inside the harbour at Parikia. This led to the eventual failure of the campaign.

When Xerxes renewed the Persian attack on Greece, the Parians once more took arms alongside him. However, the Persians were again beaten, at Salamis in 480 and at Plataea and Mykali in the following year. The defeat of the Persians led to the dispatch of an Athenian fleet under Themistocles, which forced the Parians to surrender. The island was now made an ally of Athens, which defended it when Alexander, tyrant of Pherai, in Thessaly, attacked the island during the 4th century.

In 338 the island came under the control of the Macedonian state, and after the death of Alexander the Great belonged for many years to the Ptolemies. The Romans took over in 145 B.C., although their rule was iterrupted from 88 to 84 B.C., when Mithridates held the island.

During the classical period, life on Paros was supported by the marble quarries, which produced some of the most sought-after building materials of the age. It was much used by sculptors, too. There was a continuous flow of architects and sculptors from all parts of the Greek world who ordered large quantities of the famed Parian marble, and the island's production was even greater than that of Pendeli, near Athens.

Among the triumphs of Parian marble, one could mention the temple of Apollo on Delos, Praxiteles' statue of Hermes at Olympia, the Venus de Milo, and the temples of Demeter and Asklepios on Paros itself. The quarries lie to the east of Parikia. The sanctuaries of Asklepios and Eileithyia attracted the sick from all over Greece. The artists Skopas and Agorakritos, pupils of Pheidias, were from Paros, as were the paitners Arkesilaos and Nicanor. Hints from classical sources seem to indicate that life on the island then was hedonistic in the extreme.

Medieval and Modern periods

Paros sank into obscurity in the years after the birth of Christ. In 267 the island was captured and sacked by the Goths, but the only point worthy of note is that Christianity seems to have reached Paros remarkably early - Christian tombs and remains dating from as early as the 2nd century have been found. There was a bishopric covering the islands of Paros, Sifnos and Amorgos.

Peace reigned on the island after the dramatic but brief appearance and departure of the Goths. In the 6th century, Paros is mentioned as having a bishop named Theodore. Towards the end of the 7th century, the Slavs began to move down from North-East Europe, and in 675 they arrived in Paros, which they destroyed. After their departure, the Byzantine rulers of the island built the church of Ekatontapiliani ("Our Lady with a Hundred Doors") using ancient marble, and this religious foundation soon acquired such power and influence that most of the inhabitants of the island were tenant farmers on its land. These people were known as "parikoi" and since they had settled on the easter̈ side o the old city, the town itself gradually came to be known as Parikia.

By the 10th century, the island was deserted, according to the Byzantine minister and general Simenon the Translator, and was covered by thick forest which was the haunt of wild animals.

In 1207 the Venetian Marco Sanudi, a relative of the Doge Henry Dandolo, took over Naxos and set up the Duchy of the Aegean, which also included the nearby islands. Sanudi used marble from the ancient temples of Paros to built the castle of Parikia. Paros remained part of the Duchy from 1207 to 1389, and during this period the Ekatontapiliani was rebuilt. After the Sanudis, the first rulers of Paros were the Somaripi family, Franks, the first of whom, Caspar, built a number of castles to fortify the island. In 1416, a Turkish fleet launched an attack on the Cyclades, sacking Andros, Paros and Milos, as a result of which much of the population left Parikia and Naousa was frequented only by pirates. Caspar Somripa was succeeded by Crusin, who ruled from 1440 to 1462, and managed to drive the pirates out of Naousa. He also started the marble trade going again, and ship-loads of Parian stone soon began to arrive in the Frankish settlements in the Morea, in the Ionian islands and in the major Italian cities. In addition, the lord of Paros also carried out archaeological excavations, and had a notable collection of ancient findings, according to the contemporary traveller Kyriakos Ankonitis. The government was taken over by Domenico Somaripa, who ruled for only four years, and then by Niccolo Somaripa, who governed for 42 years, up to 1504. He was succeeded by Cruisin II, up to 1520, and on his death the Duke of Naxos, John Crispi IV, took over command. All

Carved wooden shrine in the Katapoliani church, with Post Byzantine icons.

Engraving showing map of Paros (Choiseul Gouffier 1782).

Frankish occupation of the area ceased in effect, however, when the Turks entered the Aegean in force in 1537. The period of Frankish rule had been one in which Paros had developed significantly.

During the period of Turkish occupation, the Parians were lucky enough to escape the worst effects of the Hydra-headed Ottoman taxation system, and even managed to get discounts on the one tax they were forced to pay. The island suffered greatly from the Turkish-Venetian wars (1644-1669 and 1684-1699). F. Morosini, Venetian commander during the second of these wars, let his hordes loose on Paros, and systematic persecution of Orthodox believers took place. The olive groves and vineyards were destroyed, and the harbours were once more taken over by pirates; indeed, during the 17th c., Naousa was one of the largest pirate centres in the area.

At the beginning of the 18th century the Turks tightened their grip on the Aegean. Pirates were hunted down and their activities seriously curtailed. At this time the Turks established a large naval base on Paros, and the harbour of Drios was the anchorage each summer for the Pasha's fleet under the Grand Admiral himself.

Paros was captured by the Russians during the Russo-Turkish wars of 1770-7 and used as a naval base for the fleet commanded by Orloff and Spyridoff. The Russian fleet also numbered among its officers the Mykoniot captain Antonis Psarros. At that time, Paros was garrissoned by 4,000 Russian troops and 1,000 sailors, 12,000 Albanians and 3,000 Greek volunteers, while many refugees sought safety on the island after the failure of the 1770 rising in the Peloponnese.

When the 1821 revolution broke out, Paros did not send ships to the joint struggle. A group of volunteers under the command of Captain Trantas reached the Peloponnese and took part in the battle and siege of Tripolitsa, while theheroine of the revolution, Manto Mavroyenous, who is often credited with being from Paros, should really be considered a Mykoniot. After 1821, Paros became part of the new Greek state and has followed its mixed fortunes ever since.

Ancient capital from the "monument of Archilochos" (6th Century B.C.).

... then and now...

A first got to know Paros three decades ago. Back then, the 'Pharmacy of Nafplioti' in Parikia was the meeting place of the island; the barber was a kind of doctor, or at least a prescriber of remedies. He used cupping glasses on those with colds and gave prescriptions for a whole range of ills. It was then that the Katapoliani church was a whole complex. Then, Paros was an unprofitable sea route and only five or six passengers would disembark at the port of Parikia. Where the taxis now line up under the trees on the beach front, donkeys were once tethered side by side, waiting to transport the disembarking passangers. Then, the Parians were no different from those who inhabited the island 100 or 200 or even 500 years before. Parians today have incorporated all this past history harmoniously into their daily lives.

It is with pride that Parians show off the church of Parikia, and with the same pride that they care for their rooms for rent at Drios, or their bungalows in Aliki. It is with the same pride that they show off their museum as well as the special disches of the island. It is remarkable that they have managed to make the little houses they rent out in Naoussa or Lefkes as comfortable as good hotel rooms.

Parians have understood that it is Parian marble and the Katapoliani Church that, since ancient times, have brought them wealth and culture. Thus, antiquity and Byzantium have become linked in the clain of their course through time.

In antiquity, Paros saw a flourisching of the art of sculpting and even architectural work.

In the beauty of the contemporary home, whose style developed out of the Byzantine and post-Byzantine periods, can be traced features from as far back as antiquity.
The Parians taste and their love of their buildings is apparent in both the small and large details of their homes in Parikia, Naoussa and Lefkes; in the tall windows of the aristocratic houses, in the decorative reliefs carved on the marble drinking fountains, in the country chapels, monasteries, 'fourousia', 'vardonaria' and 'fides'. These affable Aegean sea dwellers, who differ so much from the neighbouring Naxians and Sifnains, had the inspiration to continue their artisti traditions.

Parian dance (Choiseul Gouffier, end of 18th century).

Another talent characteristic of the Parians, as described by travellers 200 to 300 years ago, is their gracefull ability to dance. The light, gentle 'ballos' (an island dance) is danced today in the same special way as then, and with the same finesse. The travellers wrote:

᾿ *"The Parians are considered the best dancers of the Aegean, mainly in the courteous late classical period dances. Women especially are very fond of dancing. On the eve of every festival they come in groups and dance on the surrounding walls of the church. The aristocratic ladies arrive on horseback. Their arrival is announced by the goatskin bagpipes and drums. The monks tried to do away with this festive tradition, but without success"*.

Today, the couplets of the popular poets, singers and lyre players are nothing but medieval poetic forms of ancient sayings and poems.

The finest representative of ancient Paros in the field of poetry is Archilochos.

He is the most famous of the poets and writers of iambic verse from antiquity. He was born and lived on Paros in 7th century B.C.

He was from an aristocratic family and his father, Telesiclis was the founder of the first Parian colony on Thasos.

The poet Archilochos was amongst the first settlers there.

On Paros he was engaged to Theovouli, the daughter of a rich nobleman on the island.

He rushed into the love affair, but finally the couple did not marry because her father became vehemently opposed to the match. Archilochos, in order to take revenge against his loved one's family, wrote verses so strongly critical of them that the father and daughter hanged themselves.

He was an inspired poet - passionate, enthusiastic and at the same time obscene. He consistently stigmatized injustice and the faults of friends and enemies alike. He won the Olympic Competition for poetry, and as a poet and writer of iambic verse he is classed with Homer.

He was the leader of lyric poetry and the forerunner of

27

ancient comedy writing. Unfortunately, today very little of his poetry survives.

This life —then and now and through the ages— was painted by artists like the ancient Arkesilaos and Nikanoras, and is painted today by the likes of A. Skiada, Katerina Alibrandi, G. Hasiotis, P. Arkas etc.

The cultural life on Paros today is of a high standard. Many scientists, writers and historians are from the island.

The Parians, having the same complaint as those from Mykonos —that tourism has radically changed the islanders— have gone about abjusting themselves at a slower pace.

The thousands of tourists who descend on Paros each summer have not really changed the island. The Parians had something of a struggle to adapt to the presence of so many tourists, and this was due to the fact that, like all islanders, they realised that the coming of tourism was bound to mean that they themselves would change.

And change was the last thing they wanted, as is still true of many islands. They carried out their adjustment by reaching a compromise which would accept the new while still basing itself on tradition, on white marble, on Panagia Katopiliani (Our Lady of the Hundred Doors herself).

This fact can be confirmed by whoever wanders through the narrow streets of Paroikia, taking a look around the castro area and entering the small houses of Paros.

The tourists enjoying the beauty of Paros have not changed the island much.

Many of the villages and small towns such as Parikia, Naousa and Lefkes have plenty of houses in the peculiar Cycladic style and this makes preservation of the island's traditional atmosphere possible. Narrow alleys lead to little bridges, fountains and the houses which once belonged to the nobility. The three stone springs in Parikia near the house in which the heroine of the 1821 revolution, Manto Mavroyenous, died are notable for their characteristic style and the

folk motifs inscrcibed upon them. They are decorated with representations of peacocks drinking and vases filled with flowers.

The old houses of the Crispi, Kypraiou and Theocharidis families have fine balconies, doorways, inscriptions and coats of arms.

Paros continues to preserve many of the old two storey houses with their graphic balconies crowded with potted carnations, basil and geraniums.

The houses of Paros are either 'urban' —that is, those concentrated in the villages and towns— or 'agricultural' - those scattered about farming areas and called 'katikies', or dwellings, by the locals.

Materials used for building on Paros include large, flat granite slabs and marble. In the past, a red clay was used as the binding material, or cement. Branches of a local thorn tree, 'fides', are used to bridge openings.

Granite slabs —readily available at many locations on the island— are used to pave most streets in Parikia and many villages. In the past, they were also used to pave yards, terraces and even indoor rooms, as well as the large wood ovens and fire-places. Slabs of marble grace wooden window frames, and they are used as beams, as decoration and to cover work surfaces and floors.

We cannot ignore the fact that life on Paros has been supported for 2,000 years by this offering from the island's geological makeup - Parian marble. This cold stone always has been and is still now the most important building material on the island. It is with this stone that decorative

carvings are made to grace houses, churches, chapels and cottages.

Life and the economy of Paros was supported throughout the classical period by the quarrying of marble. This specific Parian marble was one of the most sought-after materials and sculptors —the greatest names in all Greece and her colonies— came to Paros to acquire large quantities. Paros then gave up more marlbe that even the famous Pendeli quarries of Athens.

Paros, however, can boast her own artists, craftsmen and sculptors who chiselled and carved the marble and became famous throughout the world.

One of antiquity's most famous sculptors was the Parian Agorakritos, who produced his masterpieces around 450 B.C. He was known to have worked together with the great sculptor Phidias, and to have been his favoured student. As it turned out, the master guided his pupil so meticulously that their works were often indistinguishable. Agorakritos' most outstanding work is considered to be a statue of Aphrodite, 7,5 metres tall.

Another well known local sculptor was the fourth century B.C. Scopas of Paros. The ancients always associated his name with those of Praxitelis and Lysippus. In 325 B.C., he worked on the famous Ioanian Mausoleum of Halicarnassus and in 325 B.C. on the new temple of Artemis at Ephesus. Many statues have been attributed to him, and Scopas also worked at Argos, at Siciona and in Athens.

The temple to Apollo at Delos (near Mykonos), one of the ancient Greeks' most

Sculpted from Parian marble, whose transclucency is unique in the world, and which contributed to the beauty of the Classical Period. Hermes by Praxitelis at Olympia (330 B.C.).

important holy shrines, was also adorned with Parian marble. The statue of Hermes by Praxitelis at Olympia, the Aphrodite of Milos, the sancruaries of Dimitra and Aesculapius on Paros all are made from Parian marble.

Parian marble is the substance which maintained life on the island for thousands of years. It is the link connecting the past with the present.

After the period of Roman domination, and the subsequent devastation, the people of Paros returned to the land and developed a new life, different from the old. It's the byzantine era. They built settlements on the sites of ancient shrines and temples. Their small villages huddled around the walls of a castle or on the fortified summit of an acropolis, the narrow streets indicative of the islander's fear of pirates who plundered the Aegean for hundreds of years. They built their houses in tandem, or connected to one another in rows, with one continuous facade. Metal or marble gargoyles were attached to the roofs, and from them they would pour hot oil, boiling water, molten lead or whatever other material was available to defend themselves against the pirates who threatened them from the narrow streets below. These details have been ascertained from a study of the material found during excavations in Paros, usually prompted by digging to lay foundations for new buildings, and during the restoration of houses and monasteries.

A picturesque, paved street.

Foreign travellers who visited the Aegean islands in the period 1400-1900 reveal many details about Paros at that time in their descriptive travel writings. It was during this period, for example, that foreigners, either with a Sultan's permission a firman or through briding Turkish officers, carried off some of the island's best pieces of ancient sculpture.

It was during this period too, when pirates ravaged the Aegean and poverty was a way of life for the islanders, that the ancient Parian marble was frequently used by the people as building material in the form either of rough pieces found in their original state and hewn from blocks at the site of the old quarries, or of actual pieces of ancient architectural and sculptural material.

The English traveller Myhouse wrote, in 1763, that in Paroikia, the houses of the inhabitants were built with marble; pieces of architectural value and fragments of sculpture.

"A stable", he writes, "that housed a cow was built from ancient bas-reliefs piled one on top of the other. The body of a statue thrown up against a door of a shack the step from which the residents mounted their donkeys. At two points on what had once been the chest, they had chiselled the marble to enable their feet to get a better grip. A piece of a column —beautifully carved— constituted the lintel".

Another British traveller, Captain Sutherland, wrote in 1789 that *"On Paros, marble from ancient temples was even incorported into the surrounding walls. Examining a stone wall, I found many pieces of marble with bas reliefs. On the beaches, I discovered a great number of fragments of marble columns. They had been brought there by other travellers who had not managed to load them into ships as intended".*

The aristocratic Britisch explorer, John Montagu, 4th Earl of Sandwich is rumoured to have stolen many objects of Parian antiquity around the year 1738. On returning to London, he had in his possession ancient vases, bas-reliefs and inscribed blocks. As he himself wrote in his memoirs: *"On Paros, the Turks forbad the quarrying and the trade of the marble, because due to their religious fanatacism they feared the Greeks would sculpt statues of human forms".*

As time went on, the conditions of life on Paros gradually changed. In the past, the people had struggled for their existence as fishermen or farmers. Although they have not given up these occupations entirely, they no longer constitute the main sources of income for the islanders.

In general, however, their life retains many elements reflecting the island's traditional character. The agricultural products of Paros are much the same as before grains and vegetables. They raise a few animals, mainly for their own needs, also making excellent cheeses.

A long time ago a German traveller, Fritzeman, wrote: *"Paros is full of partidges and wild pigeons. The locals have a few sheep and goats kept around the house, to which they feed even watermelon".*

In 1730, the English traveller Charles Tomson found Paros prosperous thanks to the industry of its inhabitants. The island exported wine, barley and pulse. *"They used to have a big production of oil, but the Venetians burned the orchards during the Cretan war"*, he wrote. *"The Parians are renowned for their sense of justice and for this reason, the neighboring islanders invite them to arbitrate in their disputes".*

In the spring of 1786, a German aristocrat, Johann Herman von Rindetsel visited Paros. A restless soul of 28, he wrote that, *"Paros produces cotton, an undrinkable wine, and barley. The home industry of making caps and socks flourisches in Paroikia".*

Rindetsel was there on the 23 June, 1768 and observed the Festival of "Klidona" which, as he wrote, reminded him of the ancient Greek Eleusinian mysteries.

"A few hours after sunset, all the young girls go to draw water, bringing it slowly and carefully to their homes. They throw fruits into the water and take them out one by one to 'see' their fate, or to guess if they will marry that year. They go alone for the water, without men and without their mothers and, as I am told, are very serious about it all, making no fuss throughout the entire rite".

Parians today are affable, sweet natured, funloving and hardworking. They are religious, but at the same time affected by popular beliefs they believe in their faith, but also in exorcism. They build enormous hotels these days, but are careful not to harm the Fountain of Mavrogenous...

....They tell you excitedly about the poet Archilochos, but also about the octupus cooking on the coals.

getting to know the island

The main centre on the island is Parikia (Hora) with it's museum and other places of interest. From here, we can take three other routes:

1. **The northern route:** Parikia - Monastery of Longovardes - Naoussa - Kolymbithres
2. **The eastern route:** Parikia - the ancient marble quarries - Lefkes - Marpissa - Drios
3. **The southern route:** Parikia - Petaloudes - Alikes

Finally we explore Antiparos and its famous cave.

Parikia which is also known simply as **Paros (Chora)** has 3,000 inhabitants today, and when there are no tourists around, the little community is quite reminiscent of its former self. But when the thousands of tourists descent on the little town in the summer and its population more than douples, it loses much of its island charm.

However, it never completely ceases to be a town steeped in history, in which the visitor may walk and be glad of every step he takes. Even the names on the shopfronts remind on of Byzantium or Venice - Argyropoulos, Dekavallas, Crispis, Capoutsos, Venieris, Cantiotis, Contaratos, and so on.

Near the Primary School is the so-called Frankish Monastery (Frangomonastiro) built by the Capuchins, around 1700. If we take Mavrogenous Street from the square in front of the Hundred Doors we arrive at the house in which the heroine of the same name died. This part of the town also contains many houses belonging to the former nobility, dating from the 18th century and displaying coats of arms. In the areas is also the church of Our Lady of September, with a 1592 bust of the Virgin.

In order to reach the Castle, one takes the narrow street which starts at Theocharidis' grocer's shop. The Castle was built by the Frankish dukes in the 13th century, using stones from the ancient temple to Demeter. There is also a ruined Venetian church. The district of white houses round the Castle contains a large number of churches: of Our Lady of the Cross (1514), St. Anne, St. Catherine, St. John, St. Stylianos, St. Onouphrios, St. Mark and St. Constantine, a marvel of architecture which holds one of the richest collections of church treasures in the whole Aegean.

The coast road leads to the hill of St. Anne, with a wonderful view out over the sea: Antiparos, Sifnos and

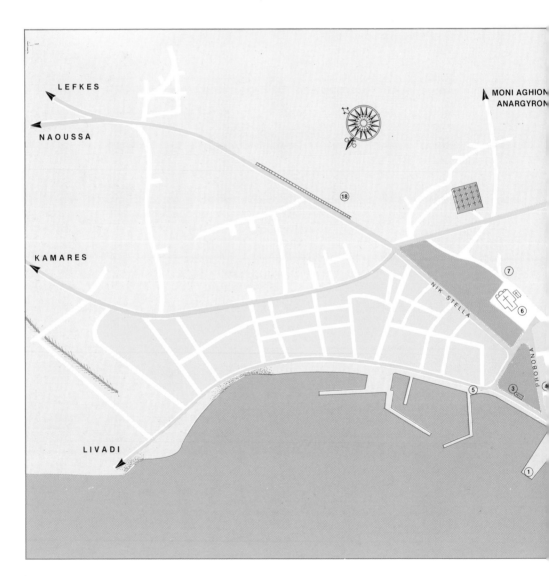

Serifos can be seen from here. Near here are the ruins of the Asklepeion and the temple of Pythian Apollo. On a hill opposite the town the ruins of the Delion, a temple dedicated to Artemis of Delos, have been discovered.

The commercial part of the town lies along the sea-front. This is the place where the two faces of Paros are most clearly evident. In the summer the sea-front is thronged with colourful and multi-lingual crowds of tourists, and the ever-present souvenir shops do a roaring trade. At this time of the year, Paros differs very little from many other Aegean islands.

But the visitor out of season will find the town quite different. The visitor at this time of year will surely find peace among the cobbled, white-washed streets of Paros.

TOWN PLAN

1. F/B
2. Windmill
3. Aghios Nikolaos
4. Post Office
5. Bus Station
6. Katapoliani
7. Archaeological Museum
8. Agricultural Bank
9. Commercial Bank
10. National Bank
11. Aghios Konstantinos
12. Castle Wall
13. Community
14. Zoodochos Pigi
15. Windmill
16. Aghia Anna
17. 'Xenia' Hotel
18. Aghia Eleni

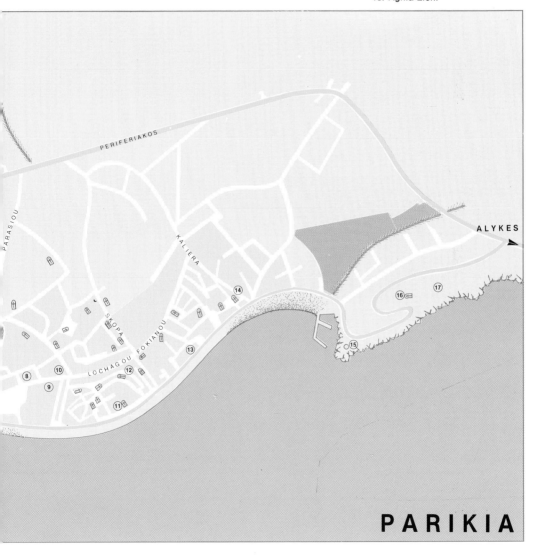

PARIKIA

Parikia.

With the first soft light of dawn, life begins in the capital of the island, and soon after the beaches filling up.

Twilight finds Hora full of life in anticipation of the memorable evening excursions

THE ARCHAEOLOGICAL MUSEUM

The Archaeological Museum, which stands next to the High School, contains finds from Paros and Antiparos stretching back over more than 6,000 years. Here the visitor will find the Neolithic finds from the islet of Saliangos (4,000 B.C.) and Bronze Age idols. This is also the home of the marvellous Roman mosaic of Herakles.

Another interesting point about this Museum is the fact that despite its limited space (or perhaps because of it?) it manages to link objects from different periods so as to give the visitor the impression that history is being re-created before his eyes. There is a carved funeral stele depicting a seated woman and dating from the 7th century B.C. There is also what appears to be simply a piece of Parian marble, but is in fact a part fo the Parian Chronicle, most of which is in Oxford. The Chronicle, which is one of the most important ancient relics, was found buried at the castle in Paroikia and relates the most significant events in Athenian history from the period of Kekrops in 1582 B.C. to the year 264 B.c. The Chronicle itself was made in 262.

Another find on marble is the biography of the poet Arhcilochus, which was written in 250 B.C. Near that, there is a frieze of Archilochus, measuring 0,73 x 0.28 x 2.33, which had been built into the walls of Our Lady of the Hundred Doors.

This frieze shows the wedding of Archilochus. The frieze is among the most daring ancient finds, since it also shows Archilochus in bed with his newly-wed wife. There is also an Ionic column capital from the grave of Archilochus, and a 5th century Winged Victory. All these objects go to make the Archeological Museum of Paros among the most interesting in the area.

The yard of the fascinating archaeological museum is filled with sculptures, as are its rooms (Anthemio - tomb stone of 5th B.C., the statue of Victory from Parikia, the seated Dimitra from Dilio and a tomb stone.

Inside the church of Our Lady of the Hundred Doors is the Byzantine Museum, which is also of considerable interest. It houses some marvellous icons and also church relics, wood carvings and other ecclesiastical objects from the Byzantine and Turkish periods.

Among the icons, the most outstanding are a 17th century Crucifixion, a 17th century St. George with his spear, a Pantokrator, Christ as King of Kings (18th century) and the Virgin as Our Lady of the Hundred Doors with a ship. The Byzantine Museum also contains a large ciborium, almost one metre high, in the shape of an octagonal two-storied huilding in the baroque style, and a wooden ceremonial bier in the same style.

On Paros today one can still hear the popular verses which were brought the destruction of Paroikia by Bararossa in the 16th century:

"All the twelve islands lie at rest
And Paros, with her heavy fate
Lies blockaded,
And those who know her weep
For her, and all pity her,
But when the Virgin weeps for her
No-one else weeps.
Paros, scented apple-tree, apple
Of Paradise,
Paros, what was it that made
That Barbarossa so angry with you?"

The nave, and the western veiw of the Katapoliani church.

The Mavrogeni fountain.

The entrance and the patio of the early Christian monument.

Ekatontapiliani

The holy place of Paros, the Ekatontapiliani, or Katapoliani (Our Lady of the Hundred Doors) is linked to the history and myths of Byzantium. Tradition and history state that the church began life in the reign of either Constantine the Great (280-337 A.D.) or Justinian (527-565). After its restoration in 1959, this church, the brightest jewel in the crown of Orthodoxy in the Aegean, became the third most important Early Christian building in Greece, after the Panayia Akheiropoietos and St. Demetrios in Thessaloniki.

According to tradition, during that difficult period when Christianity was attempting to subdue the remnants of paganism, the mother of Constantine the Great set off for the Holy Land, with the intention of finding the True Cross. However, a storm obliged her to make a halt in Paros. On her way to Parikia - or rather, to the ancient town of Paros, with its remians of a bygone pre-Christian age -she came upon on of the first chapels of the new religion, dedicated to the Dormition of the Virgin. She stopped to pray, and promised that if she found the True Cross and returned safely to her son's city, she would have a fine church built on that spot in Paros.

There is also a rather more bloodthirsty tradition associated with the church. The church was built, it is said, by Ignatius, pupil of the master-builder of St. Sophia in Constantinople. When the church was finished, Ignatius invited his teacher to Paros to see it. The grandeur of the new building filled the master-builder with

KATAPOLIANI

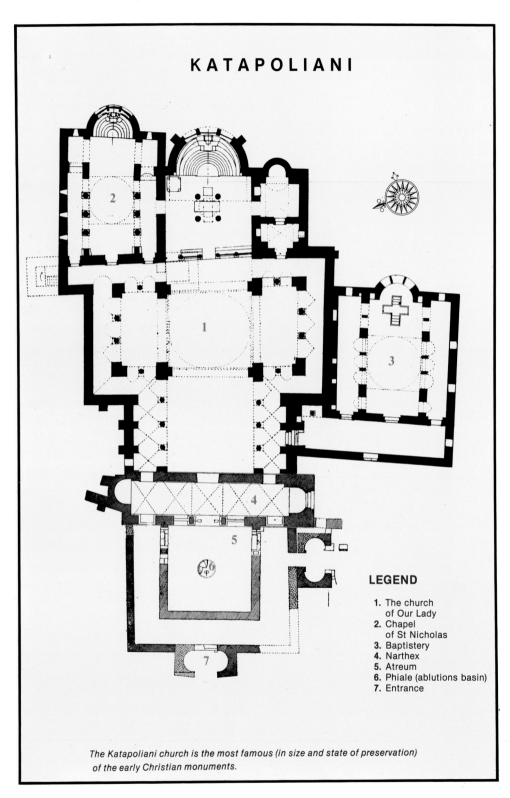

LEGEND

1. The church
   of Our Lady
2. Chapel
   of St Nicholas
3. Baptistery
4. Narthex
5. Atreum
6. Phiale (ablutions basin)
7. Entrance

*The Katapoliani church is the most famous (in size and state of preservation)
of the early Christian monuments.*

envy fo Ignatius' talent and achievements, so he decided to make away with him. He led him to the upper part of the entrance to the narthex, on the pretext of pointing out a mistake, and as Ignatius bent down to look more closely, his old teacher pushed him. In his attempts to retain his balance, Ignatius clung on to the master-builder and both fell into the void and were killed. A frieze representing both these figures, which used to be inside the church, can now be seen in the north section of the yard.

Another tradition refers to the church being sacked by Saracen pirates in one of their raids. Indeed, they attempted to steal the finely-worked altar, but as they tried to carry it out of the church it grew bigger and heavier as they approached the door, and by the time they reached the exit of the church the altar would no longer go through. In their rage the pirates smashed it and left.

There is some dispute about the name of the church; should it be called Ekatontapiliani or Katopoliani, forms which are both frequently found? The Ekatontapiliani form, which means, as we have seen, "of a hundred doors" rests its claim to correctness on the supposed discovery within the church of 99 doors. When the hundredth door is found, legend says, it will be a sign that Constantinople will once more become Greek. This name for the church is first found in a letter from the Patriarch in 1606, and has been used often since then.

The other, more prosaic name, which has greater support among historians, is derived from a corruption of the Greek phrase meaning "below the town". The name is first encountered in a letter dated 1562 of Duke John IV of the Archipelagos and is frequently met with thereafter.

The church itself stands in the north-east corner of the town of Paros, and was built on the remains of temples to Herakles and the poet Archilochus, while a temple to Zeus is not far off. The church seems to have been built in about the 4th c. During the Byzantine period, it was used as a nunnery. It is a cruciform basilica with a dome, entered through the narthex, which has three doors into the main body of the church. The form of the church today dates from the 6th c. The sculpture which decorates the church today is both ancient and Christian. There are architraves, door-posts and other building materials from the ancient temple of Demeter at the harbour of Paroikia. It wold sßem that the ancient gymnasium was also in the vicinity of the church since tablets and mosaics connected with it have been found and may be admired in the museum.

The oldest wall-painting still extant (in the baptistry) dates from the 11th or 12th c. and shows St. George. There are also many old icons in the church, including a Virgin which is traditionally supposed to have been painted by the Apostle Luke, an Untainted Virgin (16th c.), the Holy Trinity (17 c.), Our Lady of the Hundred Gates (12th c.) on the rood screen, the Archangel Michael (1666) and others.

The Baptistry.

northern route

Parikia · Longobarda Monastery · Noussa

The interior and the exterior of the Monastery of Longavarda

The Longobarda Monastery is one of the most impressive monuments on Paros. The road to the monastery is lined with ancient, Roman and Christian remains, such as the Early Christian basilica (6th century) of the Three Churches, in the ruins of which was found the Ionian capital with the Archilochus inscription, the church of Ayia Theoktistis, the Taxiarchon Monastery of the 16th century, the church of St. Philip and the medieval castle of the Arapis.

The monastery of Longobarda, otherwise known as Zoodochos Pigi, was built in 1638 by the Naousian Christophoros Palaiologos. Today it has 30 monks.

The main church stands in the centre of a yard, and is typically Cycladic, cruciform with a dome. Its wall-paintings —17th century— cover the whole of the interior of the church.

The hospitality of the monks —women are not admitted— is a byword. Stairs lead to the clean white cells.

Special note should be made of the icon-painting workshops, where monks gifted in the art produce modern masterpieces.

There is also a book-binding workshop, and an interesting library with old editions.

The Monastery of Aghios Antreas

Monastery of Longavárda

Naousa

The port of Naousa has played an important part in the history of the island at various times during the past. The village has 1,200 inhabitants today, and history, especially that of the 16th -19th centuries, comes to life as the visitor walks through its streets.

There was a Byzantine settlement here as early as the days of the Comnenos dynasty, while the castle was built in the 15th century. French Capuchins had schools here from 1655 to 1704, and attempted to convert the populace to Catholicism. In 1770, Naousa became the home port of the Russian fleet in the Aegean under Orlof, Spyridoff and Antonis Psarros. During this period Naousa was at the centre of commerce in the area, since for three or four years the village had to provide for a population some twenty times larger than usual, due to the large numbers of Russian and other troops stationed there.

There is a Byzantine Museum in Naousa, with late Byzantine icons, works by Parian and Cretan icon painters of the 12th and 13th c., wood carvings, church vessels and engravings. There are also some Roman and Frankish sculptures on display. The Museum, which was founded in 1964, is housed in the church of St. Nicholas Mostratos. Among the most important exhibits are: The Descent of Christ from the Cross (16th c.), Supplication (15th c.), Our Lady Hodehgetria (1744), Christ Pantokrator (1702, Russian) and Virgin and Child (16th c., school of Sienna).

The little port of Naoussa

The interior of the Monastery of Longavarda

Naoussa.

Veiws of the port of Naoussa.

The Naousa area contains a large number of archaeological sites and more recent monuments. At Protoria there is a semi-ruined Byzantine church dating from the 12th-13th century, wall-paintings from which can be seen in the museum in Naousa. Further to the south is the monastery of St. Andrew (1648). On the east wall near the altar there is a 17th century painting of Christ. In the floor there are graves of land-owners dating from 1718, while the wooden rood screen, inlaid with gold, has 17th century icons (Christ, the Virgin, St. Andrew, John the Baptist).

To the north of the monastery of St. Andrew, there is the 16th century monastery of St. John, where there are 17th and 18th century icons to admire. At Merovigli, to the south of Naousa, the monastery of St. George, which was renovated in 1652, also contains 17th and 18th century icons.

In the great bay of Naousa we can see the little island of Ayia Kali, thrown down like an artist's brushstroke. This is where the Russians had their headquarters in the years following 1770.

The safe little port of Naoussa.

The picturesqueness of Naoussa characterizes the life and surroundings.

On the island of Economou in Langeri Bay -next to Naousa- excavations have revealed a fortified settlement of the period of Archilochus (725-654 B.C.).

To the east of Naousa lies the cape of Santa Maria and the islet of Filizi, which is also of archaeological interest. Also near the town of Naousa stands th ruin of Paleopyrgos, with ruins of the classical period - a building of typical Cycladic style. According to archaeologistis, this was the site of the capital of ancient Paros. Naousa today has not lost its former charm, despite the large number of new houses that have been built there. At the entrance to the town the visitor will spy the church of the Monastery of St. Athanase, a building dating from the 17th c., with icons from the same period. The monastery has been used by both Orthodox and Catholic monks during its history, and during the period of Turkish occupation the great teacher Athanase the Parian taught there.

Near the harbour are the ruins of the church of St. George, dating from the Middle Ages. The floor of the church preserves three graves belonging to knights of Baron Sangred and the tomb of the 19th c., pirate Avgoustinos. In Naousa itself are the churches of the Annunciation and of St. John, with folk paintings dating from 1784 and fine icons, as well as the churches of the Virgin, the Theoskepasti (16th c.) and the Pentanousa.

Only ruins of the Castle of Naousa stand today -or rather lie, since they are half-submerged by the sea. Built by the Somaripa family (1386-1516), the sunken stonework provides an attractive background for the multi-coloured fishing boats in the little harbour.

Blindingly white little churches and plant-filled streets in Naoussa.

Kolymbithres

The northern most extremity of the island, Cape Korakas with its light-house: The picturesque church of Aghia Irini opposite the islet of Oikonomou.
Below: The area around the monastery of Aghios Ioannis Detis.

eastern route

Parikia · Ancient Marble Quarries · Piso Livadi · Marpissa · Drios

The ancient quarries where Parian marble was won can be reached from the main road between Paroikia and Lefkes. There are pieces of pure white marble lying about everywhere, leftovers from ancient times, while tunnels, caves and inscriptins made by the ancient miners may also be seen. These werethe quarries which produced the blindingly white marble from which some of the greatest works of statuary in human history were made. The marble was remarkable for its tarnslucence, and this was probably the reason why no temple in Athens, Delphi or Olympia cold afford to be without it. To show the extent of this translucence, suffice it to say that while Penteli marble is translucent to a depth of 1.5 cm and Carrara marble to a depth of 2.5 cm. Parian marble accepts the light for as much as 3.5 cm.

Even during the last century a small independent industry operated here under the mathematician and businessman Nikolaos Crispis, who even went so far, in 1878, as to produce his own currency to pay the work force. The community was called "Little Europe", and not without reason, for Britons, Austrians, Belgians, Italians and German engineers worked here, as did Greek and Armenian workmen.

Today it is possible to visit the quarry from two entrances east of the village of Marathi.

The entrance of the ancient quarry on Paros. Gravure from the end of the 18th Century.

Lefkes

The classic method of cultivation, using terraces; outside Lefkes.

Lefkes, at 200 metres above sea level, is the highest village on Paros. It lies about 10 kilometres from Paroikia. At the third kilometre we pass through the hamlet of Elipos, where there is a river. Elipos is where the biography of Archilochus was found, and it is speculated that the temple to Archilochus must have been here too. A road from the village leads to the nunnery of Our Lady "Myrtidiotissa Thamanon" which has 25 nuns today. In its present form, the nunnery dates only from 1935, but it was built on the ruins of the 17th century Ypapanti monastery. It has valuable icons and a religous painting workshop.

Returning to the road, we soon encounter the village of Marathi, a picturesque community. Pieces of ancient marble may be seen lying by the side of the road.

At the 7th kilometre we pass Ayia Pakou, which once belonged to the monastery of Chozoviotissa on Amorgos, an which, according to an inscription, was renovated in 1604. Below lies the villages of Kostos. It has a population of 400 and was the birthplace of Athanase the Parian. It has interesting churches.

Suddenly the light becomes almost blindingly white as it is reflected off the houses of Lekfes. The main street of the village, which has 500 inhaibtants, contains houses and churches dating from the 15th, 16th and 17th centuries. Indeed, the whole village is full of old and interesting churches. The village itself is built amphitheatrically, in such a

Lefkes.

way as to make maximum use of its site. To the east of the village lies the marble church of the Holy Trinity, with white bell-towers and a yard. It was built in 1830 on the remians of three older churches - of the Ascension, St. Anne and St. George. The most amazing thing about the church, however, is the total use of marble. There is no part of the church which does not use the stone produced by Paros itself. It also contains icons by Parian artists, and there are post-Byzantine icons which used to decorate the three smaller churches.

Especially notable in the village are the churches of St. Barbara, built on the ruins of the medieval church of the Resurrection, St. Theodosia, which contains 17th century icons, St. Catherine and Chrysostome.

The visitor will certainly enjoy a walk to Ramnos, a

Lefkes.

route often taken by the inhabitants of Lefkes. Above Ramnos is Dasos, which contains the monastery known as "Our Lady in the Cells". It was built in the 17th century and was the property of the monastery of Chozoviotissa on Amorgos.

There is also an interesting collection of folk art to be seen in Lefkes. The collection, which is the property of Mr. Nikolaos Pantelaiou, is housed above the birthplace of Bishop Avgoustinos Cantiotis.

In addition, as we enter the village we pass the museum-workshop of the potters John and Virginia Kydonieos, whose works, inspired by folk patterns, decorate the rooms of a typical island house.

In the Lefkes area are the monasteries of St. Kyriaki (1665), St. John "Kaparos" (renovated 1646) and St. George, at Langada (renovated 1664).

Dragoulas - Marpissa

The village of Dragoulas or Prodromos is 5 kilometres after Lefkas. It has interesting monasteries (to Our Lady, St. Pantaleimon). It is followed by the village of Marmara, which took its name from the plentiful supplies of marble ("marmara" in Greek) to be found in the area. The village has a population of 400, many churches and some fine old houses. Up on the foothills of Mt. Antikephalos are the ancient potteries, where fine vessels were produced.

Dragoulas itself is known to have existed as a village from medieval times. It takes its name from a corruption of the Greek for "Goatfooted" Apollo, while the name Prodromos comes from the main church, which is dedicated to John the Baptist. This church was built in the 17th century, and has many interesting old icons and wood-carvings. Icons of great quality may also be seen in other churches in Dragoulas, notably in the church of St. Nicholas.

The road to the south leads us to Marpissa, or Tsipidos, with a population of 500. The village is built amphitheatrically on a hill some 40 metres high. There are many churches in the town, while there are monasteries of St. John the Baptist (16th century) and St. Antony also 16th century).

After the windmills we arrive at the Castle of Marpissa, which was the base of Nikolaos Somaripa, ruler of Paros, and which was built around 1500.

Of the churches in the village, the most interesting are the three-aisled basilica of the Transformation with 17th century icons, a wooden carved rood screen and wall paintings, St. George "Orphanos" with icons of 1653, the Evangelistria and the Mesosporitisa or Anapliotisa with 18th century icons.

An example of Cycladic architecture: the supple forms of the white houses of Marpissa.

Panoramic view of Piso Livadi and Logaras.

To the east of the village is the hill on which stand the monastery of St. Anthony, an old castle and some ruined churches. The main church of the monastery has wall paintings of the 17th century done in the folk style and the depiction of the Second Coming is of especial interest. There is a gold-plated wooden rood screen, and a cross dated 1693. The church also has 17th century icons to show and a marble pulpit supported on an upturned ancient capital.

The castle of St. Anthony was the scene of fierce fighting with the Turks in 1537. The Turks were victorious, and this victory led to their becoming masters of the island, a process which led to a large drop in the population of the island, since some 6,000 islanders were put to death or exiled.

Marpissa's outlet to the sea is called Piso Livadi, which, although almost deserted in the winter, becomes a hive of activity during the summer-months, with fishing boats and plenty of visitors who stay in its little white houses. Further along is the bay of Logaras, which has a fine clean beach.

The beach of Logaras and elevated in the background the monastery of Aghios Antonios.

Logaras, and in the background Piso Livadi.

The expansive sandy beach at Chrisi Akti or Golden Beach.

The beach north from Aghios Antonios

Drios

At a distance of ten km. from Lefkes and twenty from Paroikia lies the seaside village of Drios, at the very southernmost tip of the island. Here we will find plentiful vegetation, orchards, hotels and a highly developed tourist trade.

The village's history went on throughout the Venetian period. In 1652, the Venetian admiral Luigi Montceniso won a famous victory here over the Turks, while the safe harbour was the spot visited by the Turkish fleet each July or August when the pasha was collecting taxes. The leading citizens of the island would gather here to pay their respects to the Turkish overlord, but woe betide any of them who should forget his wallet!

Drios can trace its history back a thousand years, as it was the site of the harbour of the ancient Parians, who made use of openings in the rock to protect their ships.

southern route

Parikia · Petaloudes · Alikes

Another road out of Paroikia, to the west, leads to the monastery of St. Arsenius, to Ankairia and to Alyki. Six kilometres along the road stands the monastery of St. Arsenius who is the patron saint of the island although he was canonised only in 1967. Right after this is the village of Petaloudes, with abundant vegetation. It took its name (it is also called Psychopiana) from the vast numbers of butterflies ("petaloudes" in Greek) which fly up at certain times of the year whenever one touches a plant or bush.

A little further along is Pounta, from which launches run to Antiparos. This village is followed by Ankairia and Alyki. To the west of the orchards with the butterflies stands the Castle of the Alisafes. According to tradition, the castle was inhabited by twelve boys and their one precious sister. One day Algerian pirates surrounded the castle and the area and, so as not to run the risk of their sister falling into the hands of the Algerians, the boys killed her, while they themselves met a frightful death in an attempt to break out of the castle. In 1626 the building was revorated by Jacob Alisafes, who gave it its name.

Close to the main road south ot Parikia, ancient buildings house the Asklipio and the Pithio. The Monastery of 'Christou tou Dasous' or Monastery of St. Arsenious.

exotic beach at Aghia Eleni.

Alykes.

antiparos

They say that if you open wide the door of the chapel in Pounta on Paros, you've got yourself to Antiparos. That may be something of an exaggeration, but it's not really so far short of the truth. From Pounta, you can get across to Antiparos in five or ten minutes at the most. If the visitor wants to cross to the island, famous for its cave, all he has to do is go to the chapel and open the door wide. The boatmen on Antiparos will see the door wide open and know —it's a matter of tradition now, an ancient custom— that they will have to cross to Pounta to collect the person who is waiting for them there. This is the most traditional —and certainly the most romantic— way to get to Antiparos. But there are also frequent departures by launch from the harbour of Paros; boats leave especially frequently in the summer. The channel between the two islands is only 4.2 metres deep. The 650 inhabitants of the island live in its only village, which has the same name as the island itself, although it is sometimes also known as Kastro.

There are plenty of things to see on the island: the castle, the cave, the beaches, some wonderful spots to stop and admire the view — and, of course, the remains of the island's history. In addition to all this, the islanders are extremely hospitable.

The harbour is full of colourful fishing-boats and launches which bring the tourists across from Paros. The village has one long main street which begins at the harbour and snakes upward through the white Cycladic houses until it comes to an end —where else;— in front of the church, in the village's one and only square, called Ai Nikolas. From there, one path leads up to the castle, while another goes to the west to the Sifneiko Yalo and a third to the south to the remaining houses.

Neolithic period

Man's first contact with the island of Antiparos seems to date back to the Neolithic Age. Finds from somewhat later, in the Cycladic period, have been dated with certainty as coming from 2,700 B.C. Excavations on the little island of Saliangos, opposite the castle, brought to light a whole Neolithic settlement of about 4,000 B.C. The excavations, which began in 1964, also found pots painted with various colours, agricultural implements, arrow heads and the most ancient Cycladic idol found so far, made of bone and only 35 cm high.

History
Ancient period

In ancient times Antiparos was called "Oliaros", and had brought to light the writers, Stefanos Vizantio, Irakleidi Pontiko, Stravona, Plinio. Todays name derrives from the Phoenicians in the 13 century B.C., when they arriving from Sidonia settled on the island and colonized it.

Byzantine period
Frankish rule

In the Middle Ages. Antiparos belonged to the Duchy of Naxos, and was forced to supply the Duke's gallery with thirty sailors per year.

The Castle -
The Town

The Castle of Antiparos was built at the start of the 1440s. This is the time at which the island came into the hands of Maria Somaripa, who married the nobleman Lorentano. He brought farmers to Antiparos at his won expense, and built the castle near the sea. At that time there were 24 two-storied houses inside the castle, 24 one-storied houses at Zopyrgos and 16 two-storied houses in the inner zone. In other words, there were a total of 104 habitations inside the castle.

The only way in was on the south side, where the gate is Gothic in style. If we approximate 4-5 inhabitants for each dwelling, there must have been some 500 in all.

After Lorentano, Domenico Pisani took over, in 1480, but the Lorentano family returned in 1537, and ruled until the castle fell into the hands of Barbarossa in 1537. The island passed completely into the Ottoman empire in 1556.

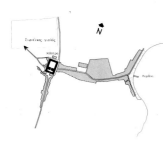

From 1770-4 Antiparos was held by the Russians, as was Paros itself. This was the period at which the cave was severly damaged by Russian officers cutting large pieces off the stalactites to send back to the museum in St. Petersburg.

In 1794, a gang of Maiots and Cephallonians slaughtered the inhabitants and the island was deserted for a time. In 1821 the island took an active part in the Revolution.

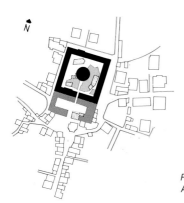

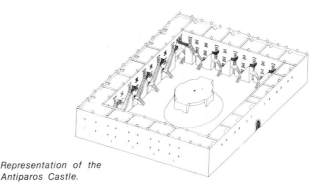

Representation of the Antiparos Castle.

Views of the Antiparo.

A gravure deepicting the cave of Antiparos (J.B. Hilaire, end of the 18th Century).

The famous cave of Antiparos is also known as "the shelter". It is on the hill called Ai Yannis, to the south-east of the island. One can get there by boat either from Kastro on Antiparos or from Parikia or Pounta on Paros itself, and donkeys carry visitors along the road which is the last stage of the journey.

The cave must have been known in antiquity, because fragments of ancient pottery have been found there. The entrance to the cave is most impressive and there is an enormous stalagmite there. Up until the last century there was also inscription informing the visitor that Menander, Socharmos, Menecrates, Antipatros, Hippomedon, Aristeas, Phileus, Gorgos, Diogenes Philocrates and Onisimus had hid in the cave in order to avoid the wrath of Alexander the Great, whom they were accused of having tried to assassinate.

The entrance to the cave is also the site of the old church of St. John. Inside, the walls of the cave are covered with the carved initials, names and dates of visitors: "Othon I, King of Greece, 27 September, 1840". "Helen de Tasse, an incomparable woman: The treasure of the Marquis de Chambert, 1775".

On Christmas Day 1673, the French Ambassador in Constantinople, Marquis Nouantelle, was in Paros, where he was being entertained by the famous pirate Daniel, Knight of the Order of Malta. Nouantelle had a marvellous idea, which has caused his name to be remembered in local history at least: there, in the depths of the cave of Antiparos, by torchlight, he celebrated Mass - or rather, the priest of his entourage celebrated Mass. He used a stalagmite as altar, and this stalagmite is still known as "the altar". On this altar Nouantelle

caused to be written a Latin inscription which, translated, runs as follows: "Here Christ himself, on his birthday, came in the middle of the night to celebrate 1673".

As the visitor descends into the dephts of the cave, he will hear the guide relate tales of the cave in which myth and real island history are inextricable interwoven. Indeed, there are few periods of recent history which have not left their marks on the cave. King Othon, Queen Amalia and their entourage came here in 1840, and all made sure their names were scratched on the walls to record their passing, while some of the stalactites were badly damaged during the Nazi occupation of the island in the Second World War.

Stalagtites in the cave of Antiparos; the signatures of it's "visitors" can be discerned...

Life today

Antiparos today has the power to enchant the visitor. Its scenery, the Castle and the cave ensure that it has plenty of visitors. There are 10-15 sailings a day for Parikia and Pounta, while the island has six restaurants, a discotheque inside a windmill, two bars, a cinema, 119 hotel beds and another 100 in rented rooms. Hotels: "Chrysi Akti" C, 17 beds, tel. 61227, "Anargyros", D, 35 beds, tel. 61206, "Mantalena", D, 67 beds, tel. 61.220

Useful informations: Police: 61202, First Aid Post: 61219, Community Offices: 61218, Telephone company: 61350, dialling code: 0284.

The surrounding islands

There are a number of islets scattered around Antiparos, most of which are simply bare rock. To the south-west lies the little island of **Despotiko,** which has ancient graves and an old church of Our Lady. In antiquity it was known as Prepesinthos. In 1675 it suffered an attack of French pirates, who looted it. The island of Saliangos has the neolithic remains we mentioned above, while there are also the islets of **Kokkinos Tourlos, Mavros Tourlos, Koimitiri, Ayios Yeorgios, Strongylo, Diplo, Kavouras, Oros, Remmatonisi,** and others. There are wild rabbits on Diplo and Kavouras, while all the islands have good fishing.

The main square of Antiparos.

Parikia.

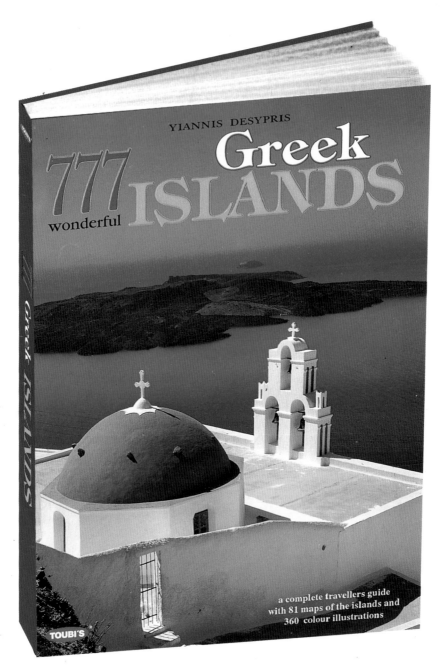

YIANNIS DESYPRIS

777 *wonderful* **Greek ISLANDS**

a complete travellers guide
with 81 maps of the islands and
360 colour illustrations

TOUBI'S

777 Greek Islands

Many years in preparation, now completed in 1994. A unique edition
which treats **777** beautiful *Greek islands* from the 9,500 islands and
rocky outcroppings of the *Greek Archipelago*.

Format: 17×24, Pages: 272
81 maps of the islands, 360 colour illustrations